Simple
Anxiety
Hacks
for Busy People

Simple Anxiety Hacks

for Busy People

31 Easy CBT-Based Tricks that Really Work!

BRENDA ROSE

Disclosure:
The author is not a therapist and encourages readers to seek the advice of a professional therapist or medical professional when dealing with a mental health diagnosis.

Copyright © 2022 Brenda Rose
All rights reserved.
ISBN: 979-8-7119-2712-9

CONTENTS

Before We Begin... ix

Part 1 — General Anxiety Hacks

Hack #1: Have Hope...2

Hack #2: Be Self-Compassionate 4

Hack #3: Stay in the Present Moment..6

Hack #4: Realize Emotions are Temporary.................................8

Hack #5: Just Breathe...10

Hack #6: Don't Ruminate...12

Hack #7: Eat 14

Hack #8: Body Scan 16

Hack #9: Lean into It 18

Hack #10: Possibility versus Probability 20

Hack #11: Safety Behaviors..22

Hack #12: Avoidance Techniques 24

Hack #13: Meditate 26

Hack #14: Thoughts are Just Thoughts...........................28

Hack #15: Practice Mindfulness 30

Hack #16: Dare to Accept Uncertainty 32

Hack #17: Exercise 34

Hack #18: Let Sleep Happen 36

Hack #19: Observe Your Thoughts..................................38

Part 2 — Unhelpful Thinking Patterns

Hack #20: Disqualifying the Positive 42

Hack #21: Catastrophizing 44

Hack #22: Predicting the Future 46

Hack #23: Mental Filtering 48

Hack #24: Self-Blame 50

Hack #25: All or Nothing Thinking 52

Hack #26: Over-Generalizing 54

Hack #27: Mind Reading 56

Hack #28: Reasoning with Emotions 58

Hack #29: Woulda Coulda Shoulda 60

Hack #30: Cognitive Behavioral Therapy 62

Bonus Hack #31: Park it! 63

Acknowledgements 67

About the Author 69

Before We Begin

Having too little. Having too much.

No relationship. A new relationship. Marriage. Divorce.

An illness. A death. Infertility. A birth.

A new job. No job. Getting hired. Getting fired.

Too little time. Too much time. Being too young. Being too old.

Peer pressure. College pressure. Job pressure. High blood pressure.

Mean friends. No friends. Hurt feelings. No feelings.

Depression. Panic. Anxiety. Desperation.

You can probably relate. Life happens, no matter what. It happens to all of us. I remember the day many years ago when anxiety and panic hit me. My body was screaming, "enough is enough" as I attempted to hide the stress. I was holding down a corporate job, I was in a strained relationship, my four kids were going through challenging times, my aging parents were ailing, there was financial stress, and, well, life was happening.

I desperately wanted to be proactive in dealing with my anxiety and panic, but it was hard to digest information from lengthy academic books when I was in the thick of it. So instead, I decided to go into therapy and figure out how to help myself. Now, years later, I see anxiety running rampant in our world, so I wrote this book to share some anxiety hacks with you in a short and simple way.

I suggest not reading this book in one sitting; instead, take each hack a day at a time. That way, you can really think about the hack and apply it to your situation. Then, after you have been through all 31 hacks (one for each day of the month), choose the ones that work best for you.

As you learn new ways of thinking, you will have less anxiety and greater peace of mind. On the bright side, you can look at your current encounter with anxiety as an opportunity to learn amazing life-tools!

PART 1

General Anxiety Hacks

Part 1 provides simple tools to help reduce anxiety. Each chapter is intentionally just two pages long for easy digestion. Read at a leisurely pace and enjoy trying the practical tips listed at the end of each chapter.

You can do this. Here we go!

HACK 1 Have Hope

"It won't always be this way," my therapist told me. It reminded me of when the dentist claimed it wouldn't hurt.

But there was something that made me believe him. Maybe I was desperate to get better and leave anxiety behind. Just hearing those words made me less afraid, immediately taking my anxiety down a couple of notches. I believed him. I had a glimmer of hope.

At that moment, I also understood that change was conditional. I could get better by learning the cause of my anxiety and then practicing new tools to deal with it. Many of the tools involve thinking intentionally rather than just thinking about whatever pops into your head.

Learning to manage anxiety is a process, not an overnight cure. I didn't think I could continue one more day in this condition. But, in truth, it takes time to overcome panic and anxiety.

With hope in my heart, I set out to get better. We all can. From my experience, there will be days of progress and hard days too. Just take it one day at a time, one breath at a time, and one page at a time. The process will be worth it.

Hope alone is not a solution for anxiety, but it *is* an intentional state of mind that will motivate us to embrace healthy thinking patterns.

Have hope. Hard work will pay off!

 Try This

Say aloud throughout the day:

1. It won't always be this way!

2. It will take some time, but these feelings of anxiety won't be with me forever!

3. There are things I can do to start feeling better.

4. I will work every day to learn new tools to beat anxiety.

5. I won't give up!

6. I believe I will start to feel better soon as I do my part to beat anxiety.

HACK 2 Be Self-Compassionate

"Of *course* I feel this way!"

When life took me to my knees, I thought I'd be able to stand back up like I used to. But I was paralyzed by irrational fear. The sensation of panic and anxiety tricked my brain into thinking that I was crazy. I was afraid I would never be normal and that no one else in the world had experienced this.

What I didn't understand was that it's normal to experience these feelings. Everyone feels anxiety, fear, pain, depression, betrayal, helplessness, and even sheer panic at times. Everyone. Your boss, parents, preacher, president, the little girl, and the elderly man. It's normal.

Anxiety and panic are inborn instincts kicking into gear to help protect ourselves. Anxiety and panic **disorders** cause these healthy instincts to go into overdrive. So anxiety can actually be a **good** thing. But too much of it is not.

What makes anxiety even worse is the fear of anxiety itself. However, what lessens this fear and reduces anxiety is a compassionate, loving message to ourselves that says, "Of *course* I feel this way! This is normal. I've been through a lot. Of course I'm scared. Of course I'm sad. Of course I'm anxious. Of course I'm nervous. Of course I'm tired. Of course I'm overwhelmed. Of course I'm hurt. Of course I'm devastated. Anyone in my shoes would feel the same way."

Know that it's okay to feel this way, and we are not alone!

 **Try This**

1. Pause for a moment of self-compassion. Close your eyes and take a big breath. Give yourself permission to feel exactly what you are feeling.

2. Don't tell yourself that you shouldn't feel this way. The truth is that you **do** feel this way, and it's okay!

3. Take a couple of deep breaths while saying aloud, "Of course I'm feeling _____ (fill in the blank) … it's understandable!"

4. Do this often. Make self-compassion a habit in times of anxiety. This should be your first step whenever you're feeling anxious.

HACK 3 Stay in the Present Moment

I was told, "Stay in the moment. It'll reduce your anxiety and panic."

Seriously?

What I actually felt like doing was to climb outside my body, brain, and emotions. How was I supposed to focus on the present moment? Everything "in the moment" was horrifying, and I desperately wanted to get **out** of the present moment!

However, the truth was my horrifying thoughts had nothing to do with what I was experiencing at the moment. Instead, I was worried about the **next** moment or fretting over **past** moments.

If we intentionally place our thoughts on the simple little things in the **present** moment, it takes our mind off anxious thoughts pertaining to the future or the past. Our brains can't actually be in two places at once! If our brain is filled with what is happening in the present moment, it simply can't worry about anything else.

 Try This

1. Keep your thoughts in the present moment (for just five minutes) to see how it feels. Practice the following:

    a. Use your words to focus on what you see, hear, smell, and touch. If possible, say it aloud. For example, "I am walking down the stairs. I am taking one step at a time. I feel the railing. I am putting on my shoe. I am tying the shoelaces. I am opening the door. I am feeling a cool breeze on my cheeks. I see the sunshine. I am unlocking my car. I am walking into my office. I smell the coffee. I am turning on my computer."

    b. Don't let your brain judge if they are good or bad thoughts as you say these things. They are just facts.

2. If an intrusive, unintentional thought comes into your mind, simply notice it and then gently move your thoughts back to the present.

3. How did it make you feel to stay in the present moment for five minutes?

HACK 4 Realize Emotions are Temporary

Some of the tips I'm sharing are so simple that I'm almost embarrassed to write them. However, it can be hard to think clearly in rough seasons of anxiety. Simple concepts are often all we can handle.

Anxiety is an emotion, and emotions are only temporary. They pass. Understanding this concept puts our anxiety into perspective and reminds us that it won't always be this way.

Fear, anxiety, anger, horror, worry, sadness, panic, and even the deepest feelings of grief are all temporary emotions. In the moment, it feels like the emotion is our new reality. But emotions are dynamic and constantly changing, every second, like the waves in an ocean. They flow. They move. Sometimes they get stronger, and sometimes they subside.

Emotions are a response to our situation. More specifically, they are a response to the way we *think* about our situation. I'm not saying that emotions aren't real or important. In fact, emotions are a big part of our reality as human beings. Emotions are a good thing.

Remember: Emotions change and are **not** completely out of our control. As a matter of fact, they are very much in our control if we learn to think intentionally with the tools outlined in this book. In anxious moments, remember that anxiety is an emotion, and emotions are only temporary!

 Try This

1. The next time you experience a negative emotion, observe and name it. For example, "I'm feeling terrified right now."

2. As Robin Yeganeh, Ph.D., founder of the Cognitive Behavior Therapy & Mindfulness Center in CA, would frequently remind me, it is often unhelpful to ask **why** you have the emotion; just acknowledge that you are experiencing it.

3. Give yourself compassion. Say, "The emotions I'm experiencing are normal. Of course, I'm feeling them right now. I'll just let them flow and accept them."

4. Tell yourself that emotions are temporary. Say, "This fear (or whatever you're feeling) is an emotion, and emotions are temporary. Emotions won't hurt me."

5. If the negative emotion returns, which it often does, repeat each of these steps.

HACK 5 Just Breathe

"You want me to do a **breathing exercise**?" I scoffed, looking at my therapist in disbelief. I thought, "There are millions of Americans suffering from anxiety, and this is the best thing the psychology profession could come up with?" I was skeptical.

But, at that point, I was willing to try anything. Even breathing.

It turns out, breathing works! Deep breathing is the best low-hanging hack for quickly lessening the symptoms of anxiety and panic. And it's something we can do at any time.

We can teach ourselves to breathe deeply using the steps outlined here in a way that calms our mind and body. An important part of helpful breathing is keeping our mind on how our body feels as we inhale and exhale. At first, it may be hard to focus on our breathing, and that's okay. It'll take some practice.

Incorporate this practice of breathing in everyday life. Whenever you feel stressed, take a few deep breaths. The phrase, "Take a deep breath," is not just a cliché – it's a real thing!

 Try This

1. **Prepare:** Sit straight in your chair (or stand or lie down) and close your eyes. Uncross your legs. Put your hands on your lap or at your sides. Unfold or unclench your hands and fingers (this really helps). Now slowly focus on letting your shoulders drop, then relax your jaw and let your stomach relax. Finally, let your forehead and eye muscles relax. Now you're ready to "breathe."

2. **Inhale:** Take a slow, deep breath in through your nose for four slow counts, filling up your abdomen (not your chest) with air. Focus on the way the breath feels going into your nostrils, counting 1-2-3-4, letting all other thoughts float away.

3. **Hold:** Hold the breath in for four slow counts. Focus on the numbers 1-2-3-4.

4. **Exhale:** Now purse your lips like you're going to whistle, and slowly exhale for eight counts. Focus on how the air feels leaving your lips as you count to eight. Relax your shoulders and face while exhaling. A slow exhale is the key.

5. **Repeat:** Even practicing just three or four breath cycles helps! ***Breathe in for 4 counts, hold for 4 counts, and breathe out for 8 counts…4-4-8.***

HACK 6 Don't Ruminate

Sometimes our minds feel like they are spinning like a song put on repeat. Constantly replaying negative thoughts or experiences is called rumination. As humans, we make it a habit to think about our problems as if we are fixing them.

Why do we ruminate? Dr. Yehaneh teaches that we ruminate to avoid the way we physically and emotionally feel. He provides five specific reasons why we ruminate:

1. We replay scenarios over and over, trying to fix an unfixable problem.
2. We think about what we may have done wrong or how someone hurt us.
3. We think about the worst-case future result so we can prepare for every possibility.
4. We think about a situation from every angle to explain things in a different way to control unwanted feelings (this is a biggie for me).
5. We ruminate in an attempt to change a reality that we don't want to accept.

To reduce anxiety, stop ruminating. Anxiety isn't necessarily a result of the situation that we're in, but rather a result of how we let ourselves **think** about our situation and especially how **much** we think about it. Dr. Yeganeh believes that if our overly repetitive thoughts aren't **solving a problem** or **making a plan**, we are likely ruminating.

 **Try This**

1. Observe your spinning thoughts and identify why you're ruminating:
   a. Are you replaying scenarios to try to fix an unfixable problem?
   b. Are you thinking about a mistake you made or how someone hurt you?
   c. Are you preparing for a worst-case future result?
   d. Are you thinking about a situation from every angle to explain things in a different way to control unwanted feelings?
   e. Are you trying to change a reality that you don't want to accept?
2. Stop the unhelpful thoughts. There are two ways to do that:
   a. **Let it go.** Say, for example, "I am ruminating about different ways I can respond to my situation. I'm going to gently let my thoughts go, like closing an app." Then, replace those thoughts with something positive.
   b. **Challenge your thoughts.** Are the thoughts you are ruminating on exaggerated or unfounded? In Hacks #20-30, you will learn how to challenge unhealthy thoughts. You may need to pull yourself away from ruminating 10 times per day or even 10 times per minute at first! But then rumination will start to lose its grip on your mind.

HACK 7 Eat

Just the thought of food made me want to vomit. Unfortunately, when anxiety, panic, and depression have a grip on us, it can be hard to eat anything.

Anxiety struck me overnight. By the time I finally found a CBT therapist and got my first appointment, I had already lost 5% of my body weight. My therapist asked if I was eating. He told me not to bother coming back to see him until I was able to eat.

Our nervous system is affected when we don't eat just like when we are in a highly anxious state. Simply put, if we don't get enough food, the resulting low blood sugar tells our bodies we are starving and triggers the same fight-or-flight mode (the release of the stress hormone cortisol) caused by anxiety.

The bottom line is that if you don't eat during times of anxiety, your anxiety will feel worse, not better.

For me, slight relief from the daunting cloud of anxiety usually happened for a few hours in the late evening. That's when I'd go to my favorite take-out restaurant, buy the highest calorie burrito (yes, lots of guac) and eat like a crazy person!

If that moment of relief never comes over the course of a day, force yourself to eat so that your nervous system stays healthy and can recover from the effects of anxiety.

Take care of your body, have healthy food handy, and *eat*.

Try This

1. Eat!

HACK 8 Body Scan

We can reduce anxiety by focusing our thoughts exclusively on our bodies. Two ways to do this are 1) a basic body scan and 2) progressive muscle relaxation (PMR).

Body Scan:

A body scan directs us to think about current sensations in our body. There is a self-directed body scan guide on the next page. It can also be helpful to have a narrator guide you.

If you'd like a narrator to guide you, search YouTube for "Compassionate Body Scan – 20 Minute Guided Meditation" by Mount Sinai Health. The narrator, Kayleigh Pleas, has a soothing voice, plus the sound of the waves is nice. Also, the Calm app has guided body scans of various lengths — just type "body scan" in the search bar of the app and look for a narrator that you like.

Progressive Muscle Relaxation (PMR):

When practicing PMR, focus on your various body parts just like you would in a body scan. With PMR, you also tighten the muscles in each area of your body before relaxing them. It's easiest to learn PMR when listening to someone guide you. On YouTube, search for a 15 minute "Progressive Muscle Relaxation Training" video by Mark Connelly.

 **Try This**

1. Lie flat or sit down, close your eyes, and place your thoughts on the sensations in your body while you relax. Start with the top of your head. Notice what you feel – it may itch, feel hot, or feel nothing. Name the sensation without calling it good or bad.

2. After about 30 seconds, switch your attention to your forehead and eyes. Relax the muscles there and notice the sensations. Then move to your jaw. If your mind wanders, gently pull it back to the body part you're focusing on.

3. Continue moving down each part of your body. Focus on your shoulders, arms, and fingers, stomach, glutes, thighs, calves, and toes. Notice tightness, pain, coldness, sweating, or any other sensation. Name the sensation and hold the thought.

4. To practice the PMR technique, follow the body scan method above, but when you get to each body part, tighten it for 10 seconds and then release and relax for 20 seconds. As in the body scan, keep your mind focused on each body part, gently pulling your thoughts back when your mind strays.

5. Take deep, slow breaths while doing these scans. Notice how you feel when you've finished your body from head to toe. Consider going back up from toe to head!

HACK 9 Lean into It

I realize that this hack is completely counterintuitive. However, "leaning into it" is one of the most important things to learn about anxiety. Dr. Yeganeh used the phrase "lean into it" when he encouraged me to use CBT techniques to accept an uncomfortable emotional state that I couldn't make go away.

Absolutely **do not resist** anxious feelings when they rear their ugly heads. The more we resist, the worse our anxious feelings become. So instead, simply **notice** when anxiety is there and lean right into it.

Lean in, but don't wallow in it. Just accept that you're thinking anxious thoughts or that you're feeling anxious feelings. Identify them. Be agnostic and factual about these anxious thoughts, don't dig into what's behind them.

Keep it simple. Tell yourself you're feeling anxious and that it's okay. Tell yourself to gently allow the waves of anxiety to happen and keep the self-compassion coming. The waves will pass.

You're doing great. Anxiety happens. It's normal. Lean into it.

 **Try This**

1. Call out the anxiety, even during a full-blown panic attack. For example, say, "I'm having feelings of anxiety and panic right now."

2. Give yourself compassion. "It's understandable and okay. It won't hurt me."

3. Lean into it. Say, "Right now, I'm just going to sit here and feel this anxiety and panic until it passes, riding the waves until it subsides." The anxious feelings will pass faster if you acknowledge and accept them rather than freaking out and trying to resist them.

4. Don't get into the detailed content of your anxiety when leaning into it. For example, don't say, "I'm having a panic attack right now **because** I just stepped on the train, **and** it's hot in here, **and** the doors may not ever open, **and** I may be trapped forever." Instead, say, "I accept that I'm feeling anxious right now, and I'm just going to sit with this feeling until it passes. And it will."

5. Do your breathing (Hack #5) during this process, focusing your mind on the breath. Let the anxious thoughts go and replace them with the thought of how your breathing feels. Or think about the present moment (Hack #3).

HACK 10 Possibility versus Probability

The amazing hack that Dr. Yeganeh named the "possibility versus probability test" is easy to use in every situation where we find ourselves predicting a negative future outcome. For example:

- We think that if our teenage son is late for curfew and hasn't called, he is dead.
- We think that because we cheated on our diet, we will end up morbidly obese.
- We think that because our boss didn't like our project, we will be fired.
- We think that if we feel anxious or depressed today, we will feel this way forever.
- We think that we will be single forever because we don't currently have a partner.

Stop thinking that we have the proverbial crystal ball. We don't! As a matter of fact, we are wasting our energy on all this worry.

When we feel anxious, we often overestimate if something bad will happen and just how bad it will be. Instead, we should fight those worries with the "possibility versus probability" hack.

First, ask yourself if the feared situation is possible and then ask if it is probable. In doing this, you're not ignoring the problem or brushing it under the table. Instead, you are putting it in perspective and thereby reducing unnecessary anxiety. Give it a try!

 ## Try This

1. Ask yourself if it is **possible** that the feared thing will happen. The answer is usually yes. For example, is it possible your boss will fire you if he doesn't like the results of your last project? Yes, it's possible.

2. Ask yourself if it is **probable** that feared thing will happen. The answer is usually no if you are completely honest with yourself. Yes, there may be a chance that it will happen, but it's usually not a big enough chance to justify how much you're worrying. With our example, is it probable that your boss will fire you if he doesn't like the results of your last project? Probably not.

3. Put a number on it. Give it a percentage. For example, even if your boss doesn't like your work, there's probably less than a 1% chance he would fire you and over a 99% chance you'd keep your job.

4. Say it out loud. "There's over a 99% chance I will not lose my job even if my boss doesn't like my project."

HACK 11 Safety Behaviors

Safety behaviors don't work, so don't give into them. A safety behavior is like a sneaky wolf in sheep's clothing. It seems logical and helpful on the outside, but it viciously takes over our lives.

A safety behavior is what we actively **do** to prevent anxiety. For example, do you wash your hands excessively to remove germs? Or do you cut your food in an overly aggressive manner to prevent choking? Or do you always sit near an exit "just in case"? These are called safety behaviors. We tell ourselves that if we do these things, they will keep us from danger and thereby reduce our anxiety.

The problems with relying on safety behaviors are:

- They reinforce the idea that the situation is dangerous (even though it's not).
- They make us think the safety behavior is required to stay safe.
- If we're unable to do the practiced safety behavior, our anxiety may feel even worse.
- We end up stuck doing these things forever, thereby disrupting normal life.

If you give in to them, safety behaviors tend to grow in number and start dictating the way you live your life. So start with these simple steps to eliminate safety behaviors.

 **Try This**

1. Identify a safety behavior you do to avoid anxiety. Assume it's always opening windows to give you fresh air so that you don't suffocate.

    a. Start with a little step to remove this safety behavior. For example, only partially open the windows.

    b. As you get comfortable with the small step, work in increments towards completely eliminating the safety behavior. Eventually, try to keep all the windows closed for just a small period of time.

    c. If you feel anxiety as you go through the process, simply identify the feeling. Say, "I'm having the feeling of anxiety with the windows closed." Then sit with that feeling and tell yourself that it's very normal to feel this way as you work to eliminate these behaviors.

    d. Do your breathing, keeping your mind on the present moment.

2. Apply these steps to other safety behaviors you do to prevent anxiety. Other examples are carrying excess cash, carrying unnecessary medicine, and looking at your cell phone in uncomfortable social situations. The list goes on.

HACK 12 Avoidance Techniques

On the flip side of safety behaviors are avoidance techniques. These are the things we actively **avoid** to prevent anxiety. Avoiding certain things may make us feel like we are preventing anxiety and keeping safe, but it is actually drawing a box around our life!

What do you actively **avoid** to prevent anxiety? For example, do you avoid a crowded room or raw meat? For me, it was avoiding hot places. For others, it might be avoiding trains or bridges. Unfortunately, we trick ourselves into thinking if we don't do these things, we will be safe and sound. This would seem to lessen our anxiety, but avoidance techniques can backfire.

The problems with relying on avoidance techniques are:

- If we are ever forced into doing the things we're trying to avoid, the anxiety is even greater.

- We are less likely to voluntarily do these things again, limiting our life, and affecting our health, relationships, and mental energy.

- The very act of avoiding these harmless activities confirms to your brain that these things are dangerous when, in fact, they are not.

 **Try This**

1. Identify an avoidance technique you use to prevent anxiety. Let's say it is avoiding elevators.
    a. Get in an elevator the next opportunity you have.
    b. Focus on your breathing as you ride. If you have a panic attack, just accept it, breathe through it, and ride the wave of the panic.
    c. Remember that panic and anxiety are emotions, and emotions pass. The panic and the emotions won't hurt you.
    d. Use Hack #10 on possibility versus probability as you think about the things you're avoiding. Is it possible something bad will happen? Yes. Is it probable? No.
    e. A therapist can help you with something called "exposure therapy." This involves exposing you to situations you fear which helps you realize the feared situations are not harmful.
2. Apply the steps in 1. to other things you avoid to prevent anxiety (such as amusement park rides, hot places, enclosed places, certain foods, etc.).

HACK 13 Meditate

What comes to mind when you hear the word "meditation"? Maybe you think this method of reducing anxiety is only for the granola-eating, Birkenstock-wearing, hippie population and that it can't work for you. That's what I thought, but I was so very wrong!

Meditation keeps our thoughts in the present moment by focusing on only one thing at a time. That's all it is, easy-peasy! It encourages focus, aids in relaxation, and reduces anxiety. In addition, meditation reintroduces us to the way we interacted with the world around us before stress clenched our minds in its distracting claws.

You can meditate for one minute, one hour, or something in between. When I wake up in the morning, I typically do a 10-minute guided meditation on the Calm App, which is easier than trying to do it myself. Thoughts will knock at your mind's door as you try to meditate. Gently say, "Not now," letting the thought slip away as you pull your mind back to your meditation.

Three ways to meditate include focusing on your breath, repeating a favorite mantra, and visualization.

Try This

Breathing Meditation:

1. Keep your mind glued to your breath. Breathe in for 4 counts, hold for 4 counts, and breathe out slowly for 8 counts. Only think about how the air feels going in and out. If a thought intrudes, be aware of the intrusion and gently come back to your breath.

Mantra Meditation:

1. As you sit, repeat a favorite mantra in your mind, slowly inhaling and exhaling. Use a simple mantra. I like to think "peace" as I inhale, as though to breathe in peace, and I like to think "trust" as I exhale, like pouring out my trust to God.

2. Try speaking your. mantra, either silently or aloud, as you prevent other distracting thoughts from entering your mind. Keep bringing your mind back to your mantra.

Visualization Meditation:

1. Clouds: Breathe deeply and imagine a blue sky with puffy clouds. As thoughts enter your head, mentally place them on a cloud, letting them float away.

2. Balloons: As each thought comes into your head, put it in an imaginary balloon and watch it float out of sight.

HACK 14 Thoughts Are Just Thoughts

Just because we think a certain thought doesn't mean the thought is real or true. The thought is just a thought.

Like emotions, our thoughts are temporary. Our thoughts constantly change, often without us realizing it. Sometimes we change them on purpose, like scrolling down a social media app.

We don't have to accept a thought as ours just because it enters our minds. Instead, we can choose what thoughts we let stay in our brain and what thoughts to let go.

Intrusive thoughts can bombard us constantly during times of anxiety, bringing fear and panic. These thoughts can be unreasonable or even absurd. For example, "If the traffic slows down while I'm going through a tunnel, I may get trapped in my car." Or "I've felt sick with the flu for so long that I may never get better."

When you think about it, a thought is just a group of words put together. They have no power in and of themselves. Yes, there is meaning behind the words. But, in times of anxiety, you can look at the thoughts themselves as just letters and words. If someone who didn't speak your language could listen to your thoughts, the thoughts would hold no power. In the same way, you can separate yourself from your thoughts by realizing they are just letters and words.

Try This

1. Notice the next time your brain is thinking an unhelpful or anxious thought. Tell yourself the thoughts are just thoughts, and the words are just letters. Think about how all your thoughts are just random letter combinations.

2. Close your eyes and imagine the letters and words of your thoughts falling to the ground.

3. Now, intentionally bring your mind to the present moment or your breathing.

4. If intrusive thoughts come back, again, let the letters of the words in your thoughts fall to the ground and focus on what your senses are presently experiencing.

HACK 15 Practice Mindfulness

"Mindfulness…is the miracle which can call back in a flash our dispersed mind and restore it to wholeness so that we can live each minute of life." - Thich Nat Hanh

Living our days with intentional mindfulness means that our minds stay in the present, eliminating distraction and ultimately reducing anxiety, panic, and depression. Mindfulness pulls our wandering minds back home, helping us to savor the present moment. Thich Nat Hanh eloquently writes in *The Miracle of Mindfulness*:

"If you cannot find joy and peace in these very moments of sitting, then the future itself will only flow by as a river flows by, you will not be able to hold it back, you will be incapable of living the future when it has become the present. Joy and peace are the joy and peace possible in this very hour of sitting. If you cannot find it here, you won't find it anywhere. Don't chase after your thoughts as a shadow follows its object. Find joy and peace in this very moment."

The practice of mindfulness is acknowledged by supporters of different ethnic, religious, and socio-economic backgrounds because it affects the core of humanity by increasing peacefulness and reducing anxiety.

🏁 Try This

Ways to practice mindfulness:

1. When You Eat: Feel the cold ice cream on your tongue; think about the sweet taste, noticing the numbing of your lips as you keep eating it. When your mind wanders, gently bring it back to the ice cream.

2. When You Walk: Look at the cracks in the sidewalk, feel the morning humidity on your face, and notice the clouds in the sky between the buildings as you walk down the city street. If your mind wanders, gently bring it back to the walk.

3. When You're Home: As you open your window in the morning, listen to the birds chirping, the leaves rustling, and the cars passing. Smell the air, notice the color of the leaves. When your mind strays, bring your mind back to the beauty of the day.

4. Read *The Miracle of Mindfulness* by Thich Nat Hanh. This book teaches basic methods of directing your thinking to bring you back to a peaceful state of mind.

HACK 16 Dare to Accept Uncertainty

It wasn't the **uncertainty** of my future that threw me into intolerable panic and anxiety. Instead, it was my need to **control** this uncertainty that caused my anxiety. I needed to know what would happen. I needed to manipulate future outcomes. I needed to be in control.

Resisting uncertainty is like pouring salt in your wounds. It makes the hard things in life unbearable. Intolerance of anything breeds anxiety, but it's especially true when it comes to uncertainty. An uncertain future sets anxiety on fire if you fight it.

Suppose you're worried that there will be future layoffs at work and that you will be fired. As a result, you're worried that you may never find another job. You feel panic, depression, and anxiety.

You are trying to predict what will happen even though you have no way of knowing. So you create a worst-case scenario in your mind. Then, as you ruminate on solutions for your make-believe disaster, it gives you a false sense that you are controlling your uncertain future.

To reduce anxiety, try to let go of control and **accept** uncertainty. Accept that there's no way to know what will happen. Accept it wholeheartedly. Accept it in your heart as well as in your head.

Try This

1. Have compassion for yourself. Say, "Of course I'm feeling anxious…this is a normal reaction. It's hard for me to tolerate uncertainty about my future."

2. In times of uncertainty, consider the following list of acceptance statements Dr. Yeganeh shared with me:
   - I don't know what's going to happen, and that's okay.
   - We aren't supposed to know the future; it's not how life works.
   - There is absolutely no way for me to know what's going to happen.
   - Worrying and trying to figure out the future is more trouble than it's worth.
   - There is nothing I can do about uncertainty, so I'll just accept it.
   - My brain would be more useful thinking about other things.
   - I'm going to **choose** to be uncertain about this and let it go.
   - Uncertainty is just a part of life.
   - I'm going to trust it will all work out.
   - It's good for me to intentionally give up trying to control the future.

HACK 17 Exercise

Exercise, especially when you don't feel like it. Just go for a walk if that's all you can muster up.

According to the Mayo Clinic, exercise is linked to a decrease in anxiety symptoms and depression. And once you're feeling better, exercise helps to keep those symptoms from returning. The Mayo Clinic explains why exercise has this effect:

- Exercise releases endorphins and brain chemicals that make you feel good; the happy hormones, I call them. These endorphins trigger a euphoric feeling in the body, act as natural painkillers, and help you sleep.
- Exercise and physical activity take your mind off negative thought patterns that lead to depression and anxiety. When you focus on physical activity, your attention is on the present moment, similar to when you meditate.
- Group exercise (or even walking with a friend) creates an opportunity for social interaction, giving you a double benefit.

Not only does structured exercise gives these benefits, but so does other less-regimented types of physical activity. Thirty minutes of exercise 3-5 times per week is recommended, but even 10 minutes of activity helps reduce anxiety. In addition, your mood will improve faster with more intense exercise.

🚩 Try This

1. If you have a work calendar, a school calendar, or a good old-fashioned wall calendar, block off time each day for exercise!

2. Help yourself remember your commitment to exercise. Set an alarm. Set a reminder. That's what technology is for!

3. Set specific times to exercise with friends. Accountability works wonders. Plus, the distraction of conversation helps prevent you from ruminating while you exercise.

4. Do the type of exercise you like so that instead of dreading it, you look forward to it. If hour-long exercise videos are your worst nightmare, then go to the gym. If you are less likely to run than to walk, then walk. Make it sustainable!

5. Exercise even when you don't feel like it. Motivate yourself with podcasts, phone calls or upbeat music while you walk (no sad country ballads or negative news!).

HACK 18 Let Sleep Happen

Do you toss and turn in bed? Does your mind refuse to turn off? Before bedtime, do you start to worry that you will not be able to fall asleep? Do you worry that you will wake up and not be able to get back to sleep? Do you worry that you will be tired the next day?

There are many types of insomnia. I'm addressing anxiety-induced insomnia in this Hack.

Often, it's the very **fear** of not being able to sleep that prevents us from sleeping! Unfortunately, too much focus on trying to sleep can backfire. So instead of being intentional about trying to sleep, be intentional about doing things that allow sleep to naturally happen.

Don't focus on **trying** to fall asleep as though it's in your control because it really isn't. The fact is your body will fall asleep when it needs to, and a poor night's sleep won't hurt you. However, there are things you can do and thoughts you can think to help you relax and **fall** asleep.

Take a deep breath, and don't worry. You will sleep when you need to. The following are some things to do to allow sleep to happen naturally.

Try This

1. A study in the *Journal of Experimental Psychology* found that journaling your "to-do list" for 5 minutes before bed helps you stop thinking and fall asleep faster.

2. Before bed, slowly copy favorite quotes, poems, or verses into a journal. Concentrate on the careful stroke of your pen and the meaning of your words.

3. If you're feeling anxious about going to bed, acknowledge that you're feeling that way rather than trying to fight it. Say to yourself, "I'm feeling a bit anxious about going to sleep. It's okay. I'll just accept the feeling, and it'll pass, as feelings do."

4. Download the Calm app and do the 10-minute Daily Calm or a Bedtime Story as you lay in your dark bed. Have your alarm already set so you can just drift off to sleep.

5. Try a meditation technique in Hack #13 or the suggestions in Hack #14.

6. After you've set your alarm at night, don't look at the time until the alarm goes off.

7. Cut the caffeine (yes, chocolate too) midday and eliminate alcohol at night.

8. Exercise or do something active during the day (but not right before bed).

HACK 19 Observe Your Thoughts

Which of these thoughts makes you more anxious, #1 or #2?

1. "I'm scared to death of going over that bridge! It could collapse, and my car could crash into the ocean. I absolutely hate bridges!"

2. "I notice that I'm having anxious thoughts as I get closer to the bridge. That's okay; it's normal for me to feel that way. I'll let the feeling of anxiety flow over me like a wave and think about my breath as I cross the bridge."

Which of these thoughts provokes more anxiety, #1 or #2?

1. "It's so hot in here that I feel like I can't breathe! I'm starting to sweat and feel a panic attack coming on. I may have to get up and leave, and that would be embarrassing!"

2. "I'm experiencing the feeling of anxiety right now in this hot room. It's normal to mistake feeling hot for panic because I also get flushed when something bad happens. But nothing bad is happening. I'll just sit here and feel the heat, counting my breaths."

The goal is to separate ourselves from our anxious thoughts by looking at them from the outside. Then, we are less likely to internalize the thought and spiral into anxiety.

Try This

1. Notice that you're having an anxious feeling or thought as though you're looking at it from the outside. For example, say:

    a. I can tell that I'm starting to feel a sense of panic because I'm running late for my meeting.

    b. I'm noticing that my mind keeps ruminating about my ex-boyfriend.

    c. I'm naturally feeling an anxious pit in my stomach as I wait for my dad to come out of surgery.

2. Give yourself compassion for thinking the thought. It's normal. It's okay.

3. Let yourself sit and feel the emotion resulting from an anxious thought, lean into it knowing that it's temporary.

4. Move your attention to your breathing, a mantra, or a visualization as you let the thought go.

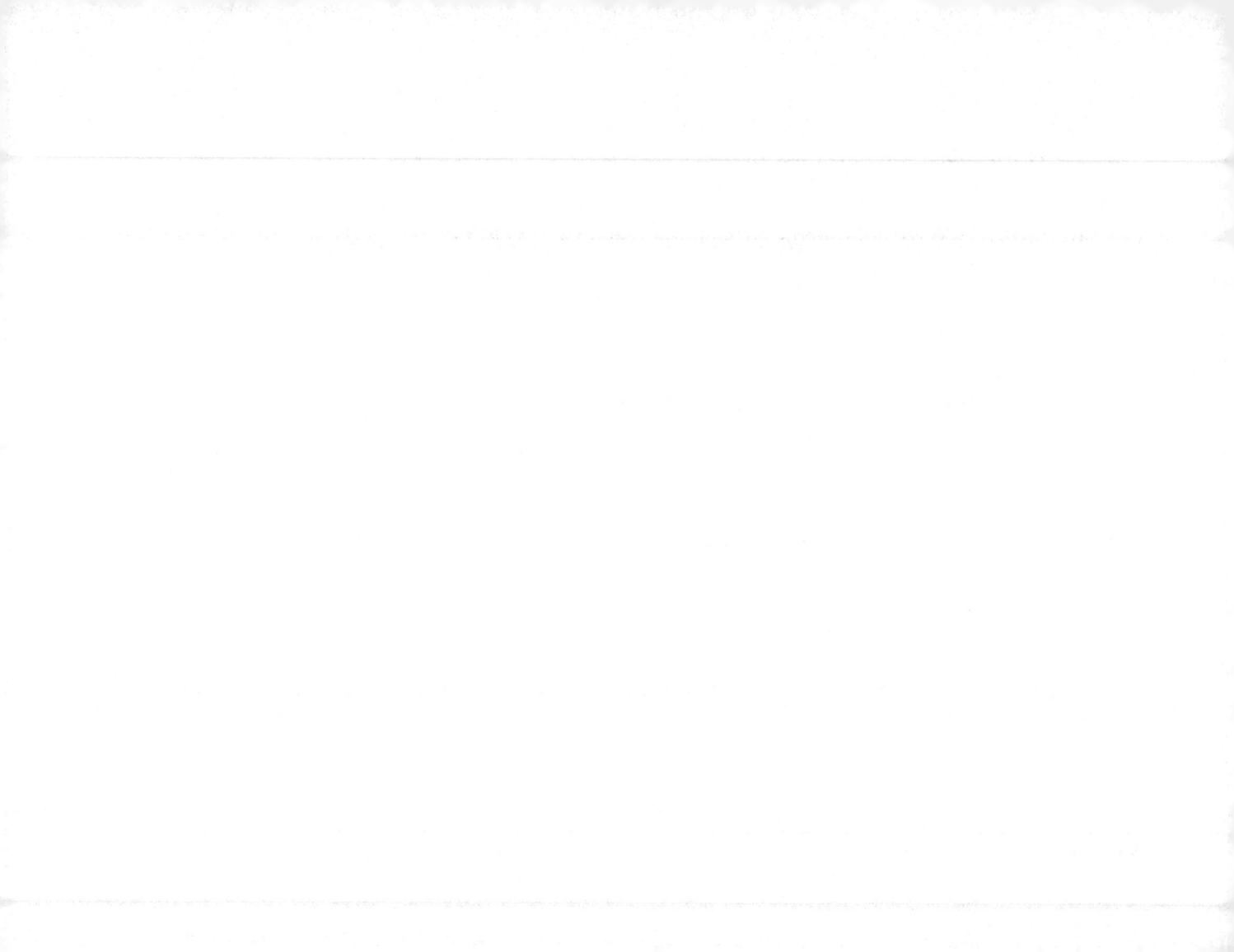

PART 2

Unhelpful Thinking Patterns

Many unhelpful, incorrect thinking patterns frequently lead to anxiety, panic, and depression. We use this distorted thinking to convince ourselves of something that isn't actually true.

The next ten Hacks describe these unhelpful thinking patterns and show ways to develop more healthy ways of thinking.

HACK 20 Disqualifying the Positive

Do you ignore or explain away the good things that happen? It's amazing how many people choose not to believe the good things, sabotaging their own positive reality.

One reason we refuse to have a positive outlook is to self-protect. We think that if we don't acknowledge the positive things or allow ourselves to be optimistic, then we won't expect something good. And if we don't expect something good, we won't set ourselves up for future disappointment if the "good" doesn't happen. As a result, we feel in control of our emotions because we don't get our hopes up. But that's just a **feeling** of control; it's not reality!

The reality is that refusing to have a positive outlook creates anxiety, depression, insomnia, and health issues.

For example, suppose your boss or teacher said you did a good job. However, you rejected the compliment, believing that she was trying to encourage you despite an awful project. This type of thinking protects you from being disappointed if your success doesn't continue. However, you end up creating a pattern of self-depreciation and negativity, you set low goals for yourself, your confidence diminishes, and anxiety and depression gain a foothold.

Also, people don't like to be around negative people, so this takes a toll on your relationships.

Try This

1. Notice the next time you fail to believe something positive. Think about how your negative reaction makes you feel (sad, anxious, emotionless).

2. Gently reason with yourself. For example, say, "I've completely rejected something positive and replaced it with something negative. Maybe there's a better way to think about it."

3. Consider a more realistic approach – here are some examples:

    a. In the previous example, realize that your boss or teacher may have been genuinely impressed by your work. Think about how good that feels.

    b. Let's say your friend told you that you looked nice today, but you have a million reasons why that isn't true. Stop and realize that you've disqualified the positive comment. Then, consider accepting the compliment with a simple "thank you"!

4. For one day, try to match every negative thought with a positive one. For example, you don't like the cold and rainy weather, but think about how you were able to complete some projects around the house. You get the idea! How did that feel?

HACK 21 Catastrophizing

Catastrophizing is an unhelpful thinking pattern that is one of the most common culprits behind anxiety. We make mountains out of molehills. We overreact. We overestimate the negative effect of something that, in reality, is insignificant.

In an anxious state of mind, we anticipate catastrophes to prepare ourselves for something bad. This anticipation makes us feel in control because if we expect the worst, we think we can plan for it. Of course, there are times when it's appropriate to plan for the worst possible outcome. But it's not healthy to predict a horrific outcome when it's unlikely to happen.

Examples:

- I have a stomachache, so I am worried I may have cancer.
- I think because I've had a break-up, I will be alone forever.
- I'm worried that my career will be ruined if the deal doesn't go through at work.

What's the common denominator in these examples? A simple negative event was blown way out of proportion causing unnecessary anxiety. The good news is that it's possible to correct this habit by catching yourself catastrophizing, reasoning with yourself, and choosing a more realistic outlook. This is a recipe for reducing anxiety!

Try This

1. Recognize, with compassion, that you're catastrophizing. Say to yourself, "I've gone into my catastrophizing mindset again."

2. Observe how catastrophizing made you feel (fearful, nervous, helpless, angry, desperate). For example, say to yourself, "I'm feeling nervous because I'm catastrophizing."

3. Gently reason with yourself and say, "The chances are high that it won't be that bad. The probability of the worst-case scenario happening is nearly zero. It might not turn out perfectly, but it won't be a disaster either."

4. Think about some of the more likely scenarios:
    a. Most likely, I don't have cancer and probably just have a flu bug.
    b. I may be feeling pain from this breakup, but it is likely that I will find love again.
    c. It will be unfortunate if this deal doesn't happen, but there will be future deals.

HACK 22 Predicting the Future

Unfortunately, you are not a fortune-teller. Neither am I. No one is. Then why do we always try to predict the future?

How many times in a given day do we pretend we have a crystal ball that's revealing the future? Unfortunately, we most often predict the future in a negative light.

It can be unnerving to realize we can't plan for everything in life. To cope, we try to predict the future to prepare for it, especially if we think the future will be bad. We think we will gain control over what's going to happen. Instead, it is just anxiety-provoking! We're just worrying about a made-up future problem that most likely won't ever happen!

For example, let's say that you predict you'll get a rare type of cancer someday even though you lead a healthy lifestyle and have no family history of cancer. You end up spending all your free time obsessing over cancer research. Or maybe you predict that your kids will get hurt or get involved with the wrong crowd. As a result, you find yourself being overprotective.

It's important to plan for important future events, but it's destructive to assume you can predict the unpredictable!

Try This

1. When you catch yourself predicting the future, say, "There I go again, thinking I know what's going to happen in the future. The reality is that I can never be sure of what's going to happen."

2. Recite some of the uncertainty declarations listed in Hack #16, such as:
   - I may never know the answer, so I may as well accept that I can't know.
   - I don't know what's going to happen, and that's okay.
   - I'm going to **choose** to be uncertain about this and let it go.

3. Think about the more likely scenarios in a rational way:
   - Chances are, I won't get cancer, given my family history and the way I live. But everyone should have preventive checkups and live a healthy lifestyle to minimize those chances.
   - There's no way to know what the future holds for my kids as much as I try to prepare for pitfalls that may lie ahead. I will focus on being the best parent I can be rather than focusing on what I can't control.

HACK 23: Mental Filtering

Have you ever heard someone say that their partner has "selective hearing"? It's usually a funny way of saying that their partner doesn't seem to hear what's being said unless they agree with it. Unfortunately, it's a sad truth that sometimes we only hear what we want to hear!

This unfortunate truth gets worse when we decide that we only want to hear the bad stuff!

When we only focus on negative things about a situation and fail to see all the good things, we're using a crippling thinking pattern called "mental filtering." I'm sure you know people who do this all time. Sometimes we call them Debbie Downers or those with the glass half-empty.

To illustrate how mental filtering works, imagine you were invited to speak at your company's annual meeting and tripped on the stage stairs. Although everyone gave you a standing ovation, all you could think about after the presentation was how you made a fool of yourself tripping on the stairs.

Another example, imagine your college professor complimented your research in front of the class but also challenged your thinking on one small issue. After class, you could only think about the objection of your professor on the small point versus your professor's compliment.

It is helpful to recognize when you are filtering your thinking so you can challenge your filtered thought and positively reframe it.

🏁 Try This

1. Think of a time when you only focused on the bad things about a situation or person. For example, maybe you notice that your good friend is always slow to text you back, which upsets you. You feel that this friend doesn't prioritize you even though you've been friends for a long time.

2. Challenge your thinking. For example, does this happen every time you text? Could your friend be thinking about the response before answering? What other ways does this friend show you they care about you? Is the texting issue really a big deal?

3. Change the filter. Notice the good things. For example, think about how this person is always kind and attentive to you in other ways. Maybe your friend picks up the phone right away when you call and is happy to spend time chatting with you.

4. Notice how reversing your filter to see the "good" in the situation makes you feel.

HACK 24 Self-Blame

When something bad happens around you, do you typically blame yourself? Do you usually attribute a negative outcome to something you did (or didn't do)?

While it's a great quality to look at your own wrongdoings before pointing the finger at others, sometimes it goes too far. It isn't healthy or accurate to think that everything negative is linked to you. Instead, it's best to look at the bigger and more realistic picture.

Examples:
- Your child is struggling with math and got an F on his test. You dwell on what you could have done in prior years to help prevent this problem, and you feel 100% responsible.
- You parked your car in a restaurant parking lot, and the car next to you dented your car door. You are mad at yourself for parking in an area with lots of cars.
- Your parents got divorced. When you were little, they argued about how much allowance to pay you, what chores to give you, and what time your curfew should be. You are convinced that you are the reason for their divorce.

Constant self-blame takes a toll on your emotions and increases anxiety. You have the power to catch yourself taking undeserved blame. Instead, choose to think more realistically.

🏁 Try This

1. Think of a time where you incorrectly blamed yourself.

2. How did this thought make you feel? Inaccurate self-blame can be debilitating to your confidence and self-worth, creating guilt and anxiety.

3. Now, instead of blaming yourself, come up with other reasons for the negative outcome. In the previous examples:

    a. There are likely a variety of reasons your child failed his math test beyond your control.

    b. The driver who dented your car could've avoided denting your vehicle by being more careful. It's normal to park close to other cars.

    c. Your parents had differences in many areas other than how they raised you, contributing to their divorce.

4. It's healthy to accept responsibility for your part of the negative outcome, but note how it feels to make a realistic, true assessment of the situation.

HACK 25 All-or-Nothing Thinking

Do you think in black and white? Do your thoughts gravitate towards one extreme or the other, particularly the negative extreme?

You may think that if you aren't perfect, then you're a failure. You may think that if someone doesn't love you, then they hate you. This unhelpful thinking pattern is often called "all-or-nothing thinking."

The truth is, reality doesn't usually exist at either end of the spectrum. Your choice to primarily see the negative aspect of situations makes you a willing victim of your circumstances.

Life often teaches us that we are either a winner or loser, we pass or fail, or that we are liked or disliked. Nothing in-between. This becomes a problem when this binary, polarized way of looking at the world is incorrectly applied to things that are neither black nor white.

Examples:
- You hate one part of your job, so you think every part of your job is bad.
- Your relationship isn't perfect, so you think it's unhealthy and will inevitably end.
- You didn't finish one thing on your list, so you think your whole day was unproductive.

This all-or-nothing thinking pattern causes us to spiral into an unnecessarily negative way of thinking, causing us anxiety, panic, and depression. Yet, these thoughts are simply not true.

Try This

1. Notice if your opinions and statements are strongly bent to one extreme. Stop and catch your words and thoughts when they go into the black-or-white mode.

2. Tell yourself that these all-or-nothing thoughts are usually not accurate and can make you feel unnecessarily miserable.

3. Remind yourself that the truth is probably somewhere in the middle. Come up with thoughts that are more realistic. Instead, say:

   a. I like many parts of my job (boss, location, etc.), so just because there's one thing I don't like doesn't mean my job is horrible.

   b. Even though there are difficulties in my relationship, it doesn't mean it will end. Investing in therapy could be a big help.

   c. Just because I didn't finish one thing on my list doesn't mean the day was wasted. Look at what else I accomplished!

HACK 26 Over-Generalization

Moments of frustration can make us think that life will always be this way and that nothing will improve. However, when we project a current experience onto future experiences, we are over-generalizing. It's easy to do this for negative experiences, but not so much for positive ones. Most often, over-generalized statements are just not true.

Examples:

- I am always sick.
- I never get enough work done during the week.
- The weather is always rainy here.
- Every time I try something new, it doesn't work out.

Many of us are guilty of this type of unhealthy thinking. Over-generalization, like all-or-nothing thinking, causes us to feel like helpless victims, resulting in unnecessary anxiety.

The good news is that over-generalized statements are easy to identify and challenge!

Try This

1. If your vocabulary includes words like every, always, all, never, none (you get the idea), you may be over-generalizing. Compassionately catch yourself by saying, "There I go again…over-generalizing!"

2. When you catch yourself in the act of over-generalizing, ask yourself if the statement is true and if it could be proven in a make-believe courtroom.

3. "Talk back" to yourself with more rational, realistic statements. In the previous examples, you could say instead:

    a. I do catch my share of germs, but most of the time, I'm healthy.

    b. Sometimes I don't realize how much I've accomplished at work when I feel like I haven't done enough. But I usually end up ahead!

    c. It rains 3-4 days per week during the rainy season, so it feels like the rain is endless. But it never rains during the summer and fall months.

    d. I've tried some new things lately that were quite challenging. However, I seem to be getting better every week.

HACK 27 Mind Reading

Do you assume you know what other people are thinking? If so, are you sure?

I like to make people happy, and therefore I care about what other people think. I even try to predict what people are going to think before they think it! However, what makes you so sure you know what someone is currently thinking or what they will think in the future?

Have you noticed that when we try to read peoples' minds, we usually assume the worst? By guessing what they're thinking, we feel in control of the situation. But, in reality, these inaccurate mind-reading thoughts give us anxiety rather than a sense of control.

Examples:

- My parents will be disappointed if I tell them that I don't want to go to the college of their choice.
- My boss thinks that I'm a slow worker.
- I don't think he liked me.

The truth is, we can't read minds or assume that we know what others think. They may actually be thinking the complete opposite!

Try This

1. Catch yourself when you're assuming you know what others think! Say to yourself, "I'm mind reading again."

2. Note how mind-reading affects your emotions, making you nervous, self-conscious, mad, anxious, apprehensive, or angry.

3. Tell yourself, "I can never really know what others are thinking. I will stop trying to read their minds and instead focus on the facts."

4. More realistic thoughts could be:
   - My parents may be disappointed in my choice of colleges, but they also may be supportive. I just won't know until we talk.
   - My boss has never set expectations about deadlines. I will ask her how she feels about my pace of work. Maybe she's fine with it.
   - It may have felt like he didn't like me, but there's also a chance that he did. I may never know how he felt, and I'm okay with that.

HACK 28 Reasoning with Emotions

Just because we're feeling the emotions of anxiety, sadness, panic, or depression doesn't necessarily mean that something bad is going to happen. This is very important to understand!

Imagine that we wake up in the morning with an anxious pit in our stomach. We know that it's going to be one of those days. We feel anxiety creeping through our veins as we drive to work. At work, the anxiety increases, and we conclude that we hate our job.

In reality, we've always liked our job. But today, we feel crumby, so we think our job is making us feel this way. This is called emotional reasoning. Here are other examples:

- You left all your college friends and came home for summer vacation. You feel depressed because you miss your college life. You started a summer internship and, because you're sad, you think the internship is horrible.
- You have a big presentation coming up at work. Because you feel anxious about it, you have concluded that you are unprepared and that your presentation will be disastrous.

Emotional reasoning is an unhealthy thinking pattern that happens when we assume that there is a real threat just because we're feeling a negative emotion.

Try This

1. Next time you're thinking a negative thought about a situation, ask yourself if that negative thought has evidence to back it up.

2. If there's no evidence, take inventory of your emotions. Are you feeling anxious, depressed, nervous, or exhausted? Ask yourself if these emotions could be what is causing the irrational negative thought.

3. Come up with a more realistic way to think about these situations. Change your language to:

    a. I miss my college friends, but I will see them again soon. In the meantime, I'll learn a lot from this internship and try to enjoy it.

    b. It's normal for me to feel nervous about this presentation. Although I'm feeling nervous, the presentation will probably go just fine. Even if it's not perfect, it will most likely be well-received.

HACK 29 Woulda-Coulda-Shoulda

I should. I shouldn't. I must. I mustn't.

Are you hard on yourself? Are you a perfectionist? It's okay to say "I should" or "I shouldn't" to set goals for a healthy, productive life. However, imposing **unrealistic** demands on yourself causes you to inevitably fail, resulting in anxiety, self-depreciation, and depression.

For example, imagine you have an unending list of projects to do at work. Even if you worked 24/7, there would still be more to do. You can choose to think about it in one of two ways:

1. My coworker worked until midnight last night. I **should** work as late as she does if I want to be successful and get promoted. I **should have** stayed later last night.

2. I noticed my coworker worked late last night. Sometimes it makes sense to put in long hours, but it's also possible to do a good job while maintaining a work-life balance.

Another example, suppose you tell yourself that you should be able to overcome your anxiety quickly. But the reality is that this process takes time. You can think one of two ways:

1. I **should not** be feeling anxious. I **ought** to be working harder on my breathing and meditation. I **must** learn how to control my thinking. I **should** be better by now.

2. I'm experiencing the feeling of anxiety right now. I will breathe, meditate, and go to therapy. Eventually, my thought patterns will improve, and my anxiety will subside.

🏁 Try This

1. Catch yourself saying or thinking words like should, should not, should have, ought, ought not, could have, must, or must not.

2. Think about how these words make you feel. Perhaps you feel pressured, filled with anxiety or panic, regretful, nervous, confined, like a failure, or depressed.

3. As in the examples above, come up with more balanced, achievable, realistic ways to approach the subject at hand so that you don't set yourself up for failure.

HACK 30 Cognitive Behavioral Therapy (CBT)

Yep, it's an investment. Maybe your insurance will cover some of it. Maybe not. Either way, CBT is absolutely one of the best things you will ever do for yourself.

CBT is based on the interrelatedness of our thoughts, emotions, and behaviors. While traditional **non**-CBT therapists talk through your problems and emotions and what leads to your current state, you may find yourself replaying the same issue repeatedly with a non-CBT therapist. This type of traditional therapy does not exclusively focus on challenging and changing your unhealthy thinking patterns in the same way that CBT does.

CBT treats anxiety by challenging and changing unhealthy thinking patterns including those mentioned in Hacks #20-29.

CBT is an investment in your happiness and peace of mind. It rescued me from the downward spiral of anxiety and had a positive effect on my life, even when other things like time with friends and family, work success, and my favorite activities were unable to help. You can try to learn CBT on your own, but a personal CBT therapist will help you on a deeper, personalized level. You can search for one by going to established CBT associations or reputable organizations related to specific diagnoses as many of them have a therapist directory.

BONUS HACK 31 **Park It!**

Congratulations on learning some important tools for your anxiety-hacking tool chest! As you go back and review the hacks, they will feel easier and start to become a way of life.

It can sometimes be hard to stop falling into unhealthy thinking patterns in the midst of anxious moments. This is normal as you're in the process of learning these tools.

When anxiety is spinning out of control, and you're having trouble focusing on all these hacks, I'll share one more hack to throw to the top of the list. It's called "the parking lot." Direct your unhelpful thoughts to an imaginary parking lot that you will deal with later. Gently and compassionately move the thought to the "parking lot" as soon as it enters your mind.

You can set a specific time later to go over all the things in the parking lot if it makes you feel better. But, most likely, you won't be feeling the same level of anxiety about the parked items when that time comes.

So, in a pinch, just park your thoughts in the imaginary parking lot!

BIBLIOGRAPHY

Centre for Clinical Interventions. Coping with Panic Attacks Workbook. https://www.cci.health.wa.gov.au/Resources/For-Clinicians/Panic

Clark, David A. and Aaron T. Beck, *The Anxiety & Worry Workbook: The Cognitive Behavioral Solution*. New York City: Guilford Press, 2012.

Clark, David A. and Judith S. Beck. *The Anxious Thoughts Workbook: Skills to Overcome and Unwanted Intrusive Thoughts that Drive Anxiety, Obsessions & Depression*. Oakland, CA: New Harbinger Publications, Inc., 2018.

Gillihan, Seth J. *Retrain your Brain: Cognitive Behavioral Therapy in 7 Weeks: A Workbook for Managing Depression and Anxiety*. Berkeley, California: Althea Press, 2016.

Hahn, Thich Nhat. *The Miracle of Mindfulness: An Introduction to the Practice of Meditation.* Boston, MA: Beacon Press, 1996.

Tompkins, Michael A. and Katherine Martinez. *My Anxious Mind: A Teen's Guide to Managing Anxiety and Panic.* Washington, D.C., Magination Press, 2009.

Tomiyama, J., et al. 2010. "Low Calorie Dieting Increases Cortisol." *Psychosomatic Medicine. 72: 357- 64.*

Mayo Clinic Staff. Depression and Anxiety: Exercise Eases Symptoms. Mayo Clinic. https://www.mayoclinic.org/diseases-conditions/depression/in-depth/depression-and-exercise/art-20046495. Published September 27, 2017. Accessed March 13, 2021.

Mayo Clinic Staff. Exercise and stress: Get moving to manage stress. Mayo Clinic. https://www.mayoclinic.org/healthy-lifestyle/stress-management/in-depth/exercise-and-stress/art-20044469. Published August 18, 2020. Accessed March 7, 2021.

Michael Scullin. The effects of bedtime writing on difficulty falling asleep: A polysomnographic study comparing to-do lists and completed activity lists 2018 Jan;147(1):139-146. doi: 10.1037/xge0000374. Epub 2017 Oct 23.

ACKNOWLEDGMENTS

Many thanks to Robin Yeganeh, Ph.D., Assistant Clinical Professor at UC Berkeley and founder of Psystrong® Consulting and the Cognitive Behavior Therapy & Mindfulness Center in California, who skillfully and patiently taught me the CBT concepts in this book during the months that followed an unexpected and debilitating experience of panic and anxiety.

ABOUT THE AUTHOR

Born and raised in Northern Minnesota, Brenda Rose went on to get an accounting degree from the University of North Carolina at Wilmington followed by an MBA from the Carlson School of Management, a business school at the University of Minnesota. With a CPA in hand, she started her career in public accounting in Baltimore and shifted into consumer products marketing in Minneapolis. From there, she dove headfirst into motherhood, raising her four kids in California. Since 2006, she has been involved in executive finance recruitment and helping CPA firms build and operate teams of consultants serving the national middle-market and M&A ecosystem. She enjoys staying active in the beautiful California climate, continues to pursue her lifelong hobby of violin performance, and cherishes every second with her family. Encouraging others is her passion and the reason why she wrote this book. You can find further content and reach out to her at intentionalthinking.com.

Made in the USA
Middletown, DE
03 March 2022